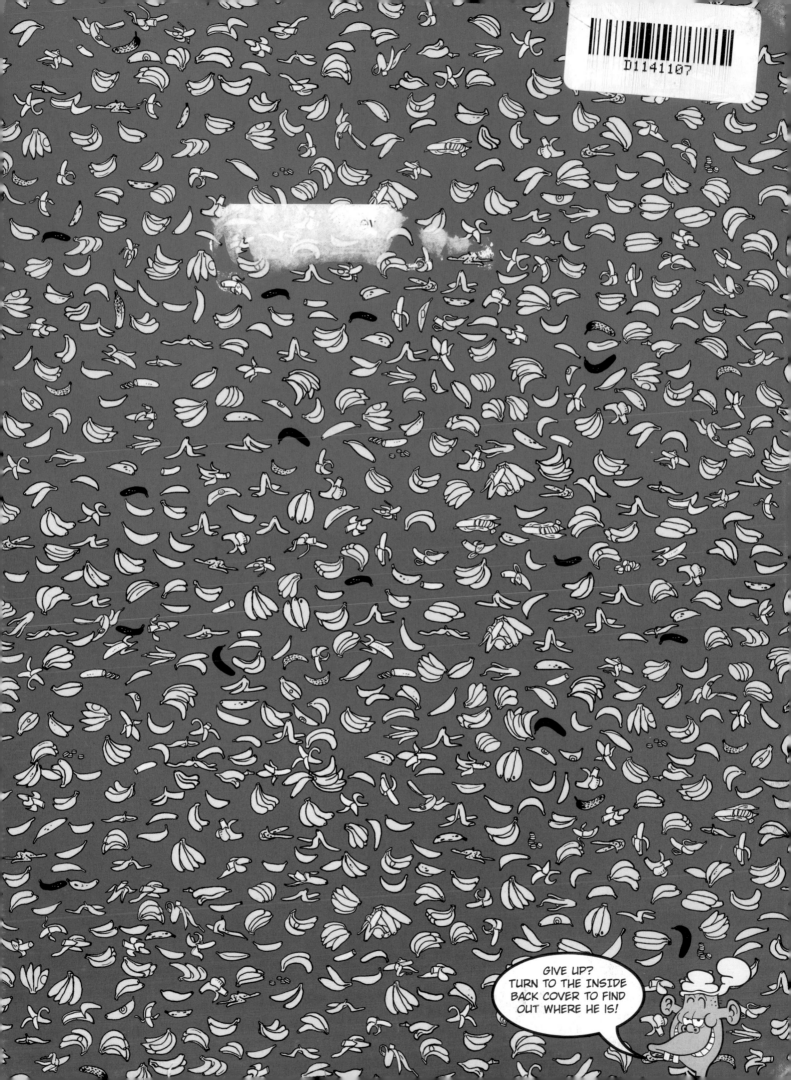

GIVE UP?
TURN TO THE INSIDE
BACK COVER TO FIND
OUT WHERE HE IS!

PUFFIN BOOKS
Published by the Penguin Group: London,
New York, Australia, Canada, India, Ireland, New Zealand
and South Africa
Penguin Books Ltd, Registered Offices: 80 Strand, London
WC2R 0RL, England

puffinbooks.com

First published 2014
001
Illustrated by Wilbur Dawbarn
Copyright © DC Thomson & Co. Ltd., 2014
The Beano ® ©, Dennis the Menace and associated
characters TM and
© DC Thomson & Co. Ltd. 2014

Made and printed in China

ISBN: 978 0 141 35209 1

CONTENTS

Spot the Menace! 8

School Dinners 10

Bats and Balls 12

School's Out! 14

Fun in the Sun 16

Fairground Frolics 18

Welcome to Beanotown 20

Bunkerton Castle 22

Camping Capers 24

The Greatest Show in Beanotown! ..26

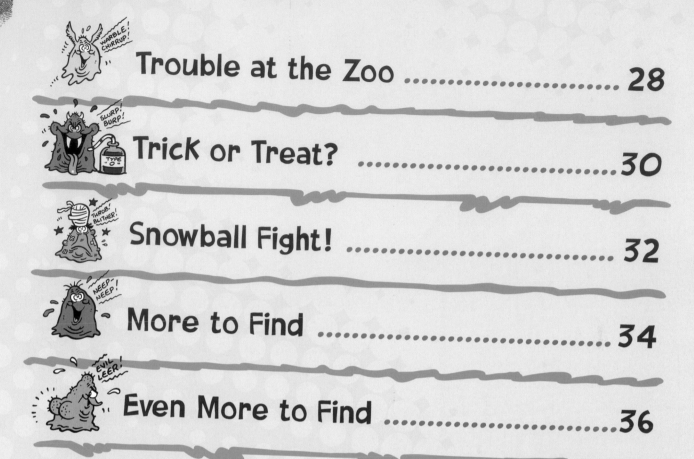

Trouble at the Zoo 28

Trick or Treat? 30

Snowball Fight! 32

More to Find 34

Even More to Find 36

SPLOSH!

CHAOS

WHUMP!

PHAAART!

SPOT THE MENACE!

This is DENNIS. He's a menace.

This is MRS CREECHER. She's a teacher.

In the wild, they're natural enemies. The menace annoys the teacher, and the teacher nags the menace. It's a dance as old as time. But why can't they just get along? Well, sometimes it's because the menace has poured warm custard down the back of the teacher's pants. Other times, it's because the teacher keeps going on about maths or something.

OVER HERE!

EWSAGENT

EVERYONE WE KNOW ...

LOVES THE BEANO!

On this particular occasion, it's because the menace hasn't done his homework. It's not his fault, honest. He would have done it, but he accidentally stuffed it down the toilet and flushed six times. Now, in a heroic effort to keep the peace, Dennis has decided to hide out until it all blows over. Mrs Creecher isn't happy with that, though, so she's searching all over for him.

Can you prove you're better than a teacher by finding Dennis before she does? Go on, give it a try. You owe it to your fellow menaces!

How to use this book

Dennis knows all the best places in Beanotown for hiding, so your tiny peepers will need to work their very hardest if they're going to find him! While you're looking for him, you might also want to keep an eye out for these guys . . .

MRS CREECHER
Boo! Hiss! Thrrrp!

GNASHER
Dennis's dog (hooray!)

GNIPPER
Son of Gnasher!

Think you've found everyone?

Head over to pages 34–37, where you'll find loads more stuff to look for, including Squelchy Things a-plenty! SQUELCH.

FAIRGROUND FROLICS

Come to Beanoland! It's the most fun you can have for £48.50. What's more, there have only been seven serious accidents in the last four months. From white-knuckle rides to three-hour-long queues, there's nothing they haven't thought of!

GHOST TRAIN

TROUBLE AT THE ZOO

Lions! Tigers! Bears! Some sort of deer! A dark tank with loads of plants in it that might not actually contain an animal but no one seems entirely sure! If you want to see all manner of incredible beasts, there's nowhere better to go than Beanotown's very own zoo.

29

MORE TO FIND

SCHOOL DINNERS (page 10)

- Ten cans of Windy Beans
- A boy eating a girl's hair
- Two children sharing some spaghetti
- An eyeball on the end of a fork
- A scuttling spider

- Pie Face enjoying his perfect lunch
- A girl spinning a plate on the end of her finger
- Bananagirl looking disappointed with what's in her lunch box
- Smiffy tucking in to Spotty's tie
- A Squelchy Thing on a plate

BATS AND BALLS (page 12)

- Ten shuttlecocks
- Smiffy, looking suspiciously like he might be in the wrong kit
- A snake
- A boy reading his copy of The Beano while he exercises
- A boy checking his mobile phone

- A Bash Street Kid being used for dribbling practice
- A mole receiving a knock on the head
- A group of familiar-looking judges
- Two parents having an argument
- A Squelchy Thing wearing an American football helmet

SCHOOL'S OUT! (page 14)

- Ten pencils
- A boy pumping up his bicycle tyre
- A set of false teeth
- Wilfrid hitching a ride on a toy aeroplane
- A giant tentacle

- A child escaping through a hole in a wall
- A boy struggling to carry an extremely heavy school bag
- Someone digging their way out of the playground
- A paper aeroplane lodged in someone's hair
- A skipping Squelchy Thing

FUN IN THE SUN (page 16)

- [ ] Ten sea shells
- [ ] A girl who has just hurt her foot on a sharp shell
- [ ] A man buried up to his neck in the sand
- [ ] An elephant's trunk
- [ ] Tricky Dicky swapping sun cream for tomato ketchup

- [ ] A seagull carrying a hot dog
- [ ] Les Pretend dressed up as a crab
- [ ] A boy with no clothes on
- [ ] Winston the Cat wearing a snorkel and armbands
- [ ] A Squelchy Thing wearing a handkerchief on its head

FAIRGROUND FROLICS (page 18)

- [ ] Twelve donuts (one of which doesn't have a hole!)
- [ ] Two bats
- [ ] A vulture looking forward to its next meal
- [ ] A devilish ride attendant
- [ ] A man wearing candyfloss where his wig once was

- [ ] Rasher, Dennis's pet porker
- [ ] A small boy with a big teddy bear
- [ ] Roger the Dodger, looking taller than usual
- [ ] A very short man holding hands with a very tall woman
- [ ] A Squelchy Thing tied to a balloon

WELCOME TO BEANOTOWN (page 20)

- [ ] Ten traffic cones
- [ ] A Beanotown resident being held hostage
- [ ] An old lady who won't give up her handbag without a fight
- [ ] A confused coffee-lover
- [ ] A go-kart that has been clamped

- [ ] A firework in a glass bottle
- [ ] A dog with a yo-yo tied to its tail
- [ ] Erbert sporting an impressive new pair of glasses
- [ ] Wilfred enjoying a duck's eye view of the town
- [ ] A Squelchy Thing on a skateboard

BUNKERTON CASTLE (page 22)

- [ ] Ten £100 notes
- [ ] The Queen enjoying the latest issue of The Beano
- [ ] A Bash Street Kid wielding a sword
- [ ] A whoopee cushion
- [ ] A pair of eyes peeking out from a loose stone slab
- [ ] A girl with a heart on her dress
- [ ] A dog patting another dog on the head
- [ ] A penguin
- [ ] A waiter helping himself to some food
- [ ] An upper-class Squelchy Thing wearing a top hat and monocle

CAMPING CAPERS (page 24)

- [ ] Ten hazelnuts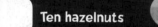
- [ ] Baby Bea causing a stink
- [ ] A TV survival expert
- [ ] Erbert with some new friends
- [ ] A cowboy
- [ ] A bird that has lost its feathers
- [ ] A boy carrying a fishing rod with a fish dangling from the end
- [ ] A mouse being disturbed in the bath
- [ ] A boy watching a snail
- [ ] A Squelchy Thing wearing an explorer's hat

THE GREATEST SHOW IN BEANOTOWN! (page 26)

- [ ] Ten juggler's skittles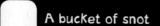
- [ ] Two children fighting with each other
- [ ] A bucket of snot
- [ ] A man using a long straw to steal someone else's drink
- [ ] Santa Claus, the Devil and the Easter Bunny
- [ ] A boy balancing an apple on his nose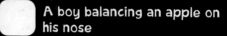
- [ ] Desperate Dan
- [ ] A tortoise wearing a clown's hat and red nose
- [ ] A contortionist reading The Beano
- [ ] A Squelchy Thing leaping through a ring of fire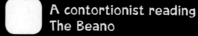

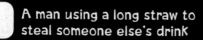

TROUBLE AT THE ZOO (page 28)

- [ ] Ten parrots (one has an eyepatch and a wooden leg)
- [ ] Ball Boy doing Keepy-ups with an armadillo
- [ ] A baby crocodile hatching out of its egg
- [ ] A turtle showing off its martial arts skills
- [ ] A boy dressed as a rabbit

- [ ] Lord Snooty being given a personal tour
- [ ] Eric stretching for a banana
- [ ] A Bash Street Kid taking a dip
- [ ] Babyface Finlayson hitching a ride
- [ ] A Squelchy Thing wearing a safari hat

TRICK OR TREAT? (page 30)

- [ ] Ten vampire bats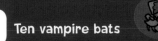
- [ ] A wicked-looking garden gnome
- [ ] A pumpkin pram
- [ ] Smiffy dressed as Santa Claus
- [ ] Pearman!

- [ ] The Nibblers having some plant problems
- [ ] A monster hiding under a bed
- [ ] Les Pretend dressed as his own gravestone
- [ ] The feet of a flattened witch
- [ ] Count Squelchy

SNOWBALL FIGHT! (page 32)

- [ ] Twelve robins
- [ ] An inappropriately dressed Little Plum
- [ ] A devilish snow angel
- [ ] The Nibblers decorating their Christmas Tree
- [ ] A sleeping cat

- [ ] A clown's reflection
- [ ] A boy wrapped in cotton wool
- [ ] Five children attempting to ride one sledge
- [ ] A girl with a REALLY tall hat
- [ ] A Squelchy Thing wearing a Santa hat